EASY GUITAR
WITH NOTES & TAB

SELECTIONS FROM

O BROTHER, WHERE ART THOU?

Artwork and photos courtesy of Touchstone Pictures

ISBN 978-0-634-04903-3

HAL•LEONARD®
CORPORATION

7777 W. BLUEMOUND RD. P.O. BOX 13819 MILWAUKEE, WI 53213

Visit Hal Leonard Online at
www.halleonard.com

CONTENTS

STRUM AND PICK PATTERNS

This chart contains the suggested strum and pick patterns that are referred to by number at the beginning
of each song in this book. The symbols ⊓ and v in the strum patterns refer to down and up strokes, respectively.
The letters in the pick patterns indicate which right-hand fingers plays which strings.

p = thumb
i = index finger
m = middle finger
a = ring finger

For example; Pick Pattern 2
is played: thumb - index - middle - ring

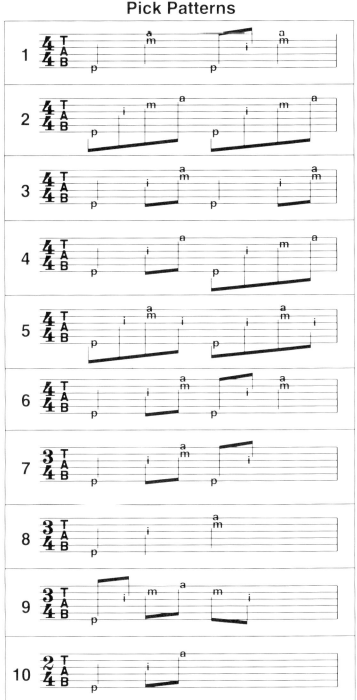

Strum Patterns

Pick Patterns

You can use the 3/4 Strum or Pick Patterns in songs written in compound meter (6/8, 9/8, 12/8, etc.).
For example, you can accompany a song in 6/8 by playing the 3/4 pattern twice in each measure.
The 4/4 Strum and Pick Patterns can be used for songs written in cut time (¢) by doubling the note
time values in the patterns. Each pattern would therefore last two measures in cut time.

The Big Rock Candy Mountain

Words, Music and Arrangement by Harry K. McClintock

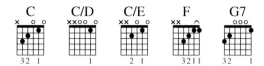

Strum Pattern: 3, 4
Pick Pattern: 3, 4

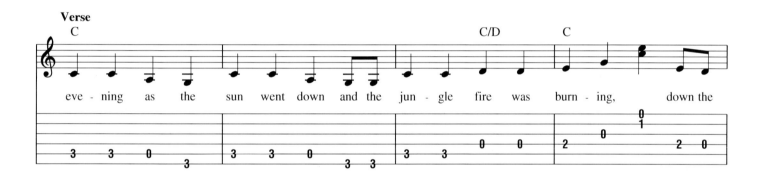

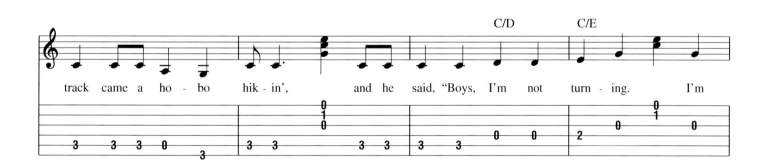

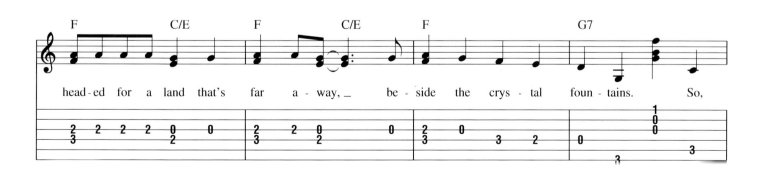

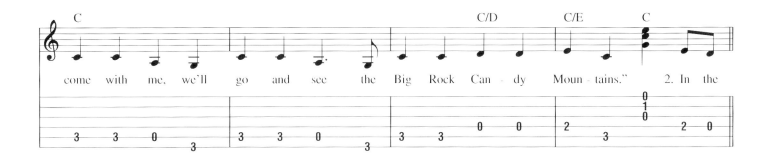

come with me, we'll go and see the Big Rock Can - dy Moun - tains." 2. In the

Verse

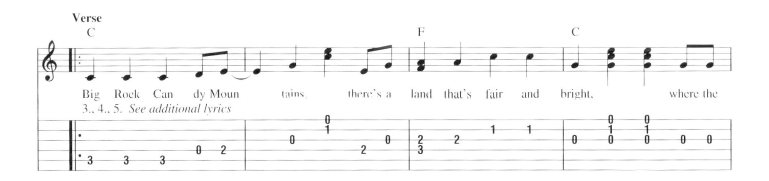

Big Rock Can - dy Moun - tains, there's a land that's fair and bright, where the
3., 4., 5. *See additional lyrics*

hand - outs grow on bush - es and you sleep out ev - 'ry night; where the

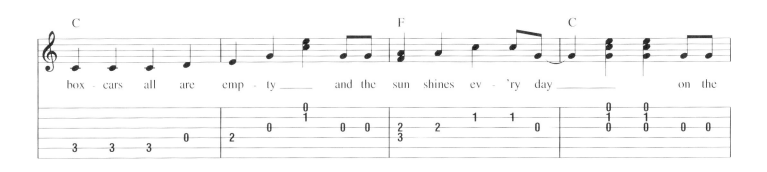

box - cars all are emp - ty _____ and the sun shines ev - 'ry day _____ on the

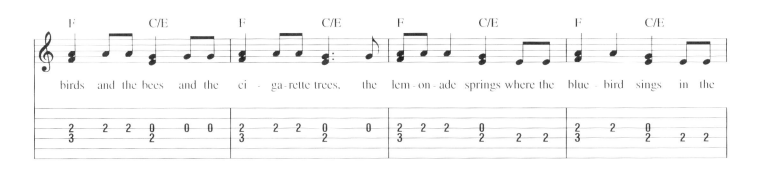

birds and the bees and the ci - ga - rette trees, the lem - on - ade springs where the blue - bird sings in the

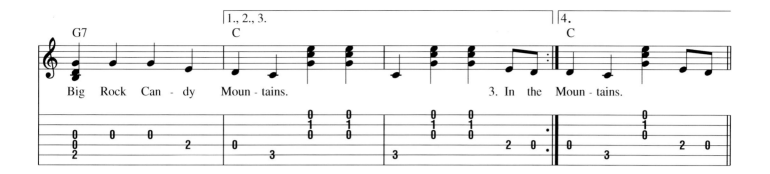

Outro

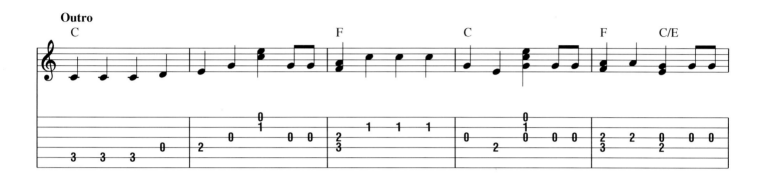

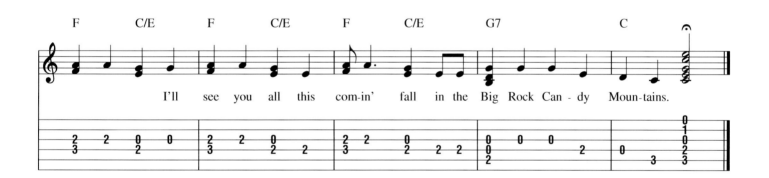

I'll see you all this com-in' fall in the Big Rock Can - dy Moun-tains.

Additional Lyrics

3. In the Big Rock Candy Mountains,
   All the cops have wooden legs,
   And the bulldogs all have rubber teeth
   And the hens lay soft-boiled eggs.
   The farmers' trees are full of fruit
   And the barns are full of hay.
   Oh, I'm bound to go where there ain't no snow,
   Where the rain don't fall, and the wind don't blow
   In the Big Rock Candy Mountains.

4. In the Big Rock Candy Mountains,
   You never change your socks,
   And the little streams of alcohol
   Come a-trickling down the rocks.
   The brakemen have to tip their hats
   And the railroad bulls are blind.
   There's a lake of stew and whiskey, too.
   You can paddle all around 'em in a big canoe
   In the Big Rock Candy Mountains.

5. In the Big Rock Candy Mountains,
   The jails are made of tin,
   And you can walk right out again
   As soon as you are in.
   There ain't no short-handed shovels,
   No axes, saws, or picks.
   I'm a-goin' to stay where you sleep all day,
   Where they heap the turk that invented work
   In the Big Rock Candy Mountains.

You Are My Sunshine

Words and Music by Jimmie Davis and Charles Mitchell

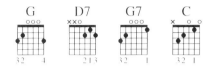

Strum Pattern: 3, 4
Pick Pattern: 3, 4

Intro
Moderately

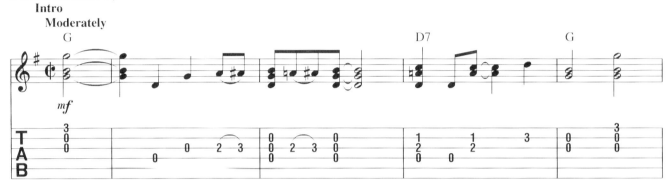

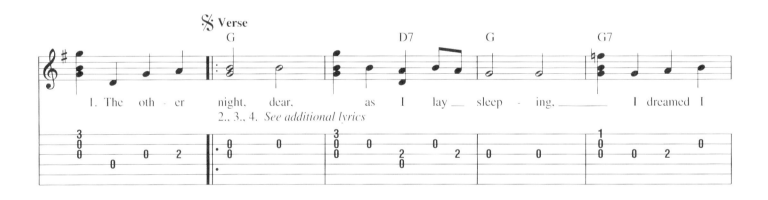

1. The oth - er night, dear, as I lay sleep - ing, _____ I dreamed I
2., 3., 4. *See additional lyrics*

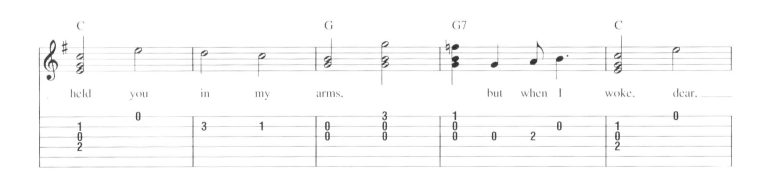

held you in my arms, but when I woke, dear, _____

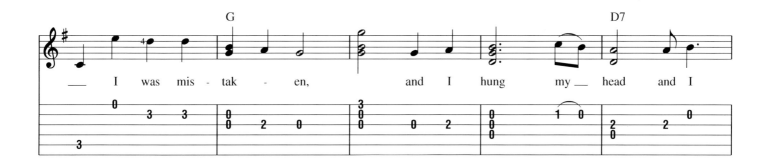

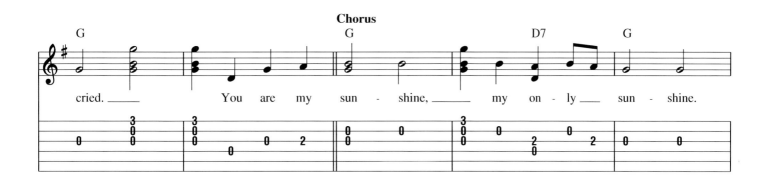

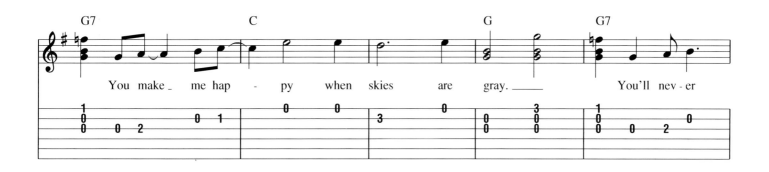

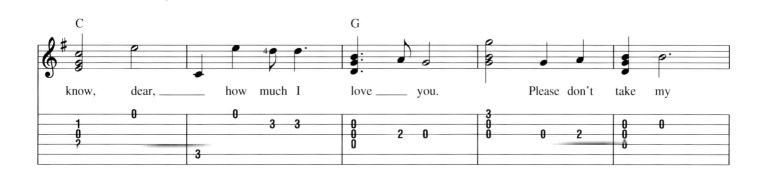

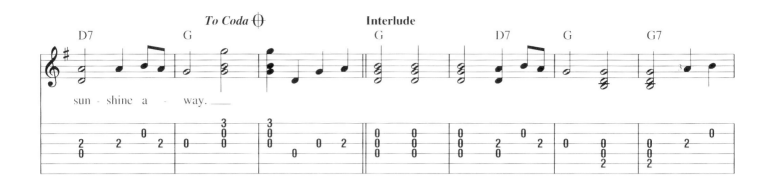

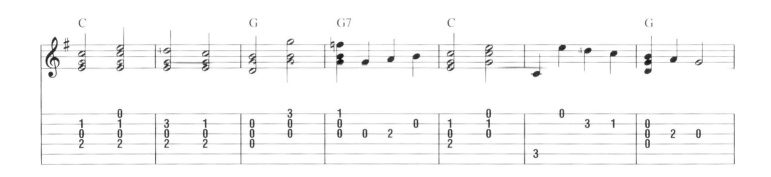

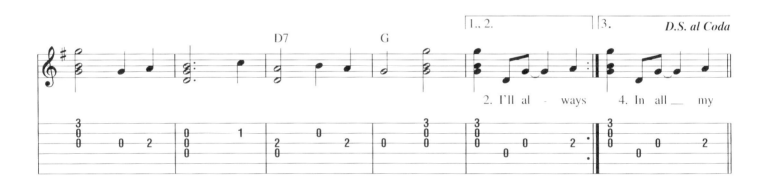

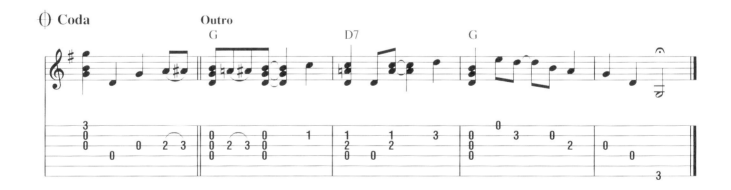

Additional Lyrics

2. I'll always love you and make you happy
   If you will only say the same.
   But if you leave me and love another
   You'll regret it all someday.

3. You told me once, dear, you really loved me
   And no one could come between,
   But now you've left me to love another.
   You have shattered all of my dreams.

4. In all my dreams, dear, you seem to leave me.
   When I awake my poor heart pains.
   So won't you come back and make me happy?
   I'll forgive, dear, I'll take all the blame.

Keep on the Sunny Side

Words and Music by A.P. Carter

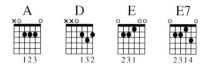

Strum Pattern: 3, 4
Pick Pattern: 1, 3

Intro

Moderately

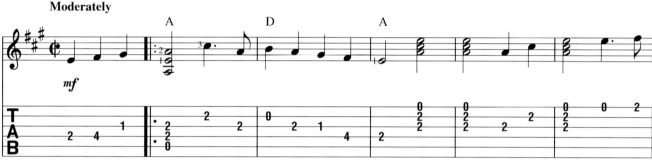

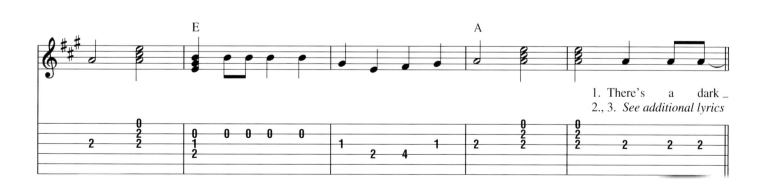

1. There's a dark _
2., 3. *See additional lyrics*

Verse

_____ and a trou - bled side of life, _____ but there's _ a bright _ and a

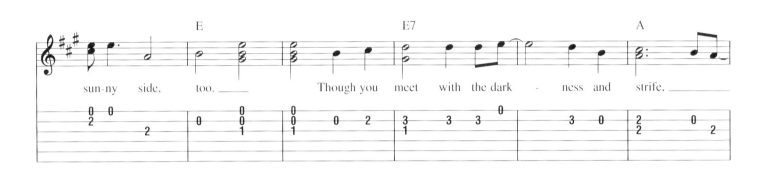

sun - ny side, too. _____ Though you meet with the dark - ness and strife, _____

_____ the sun - ny side _ you al - so _ may view. _____

Chorus

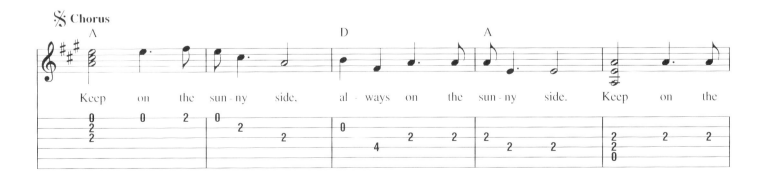

Keep on the sun - ny side, al - ways on the sun - ny side. Keep on the

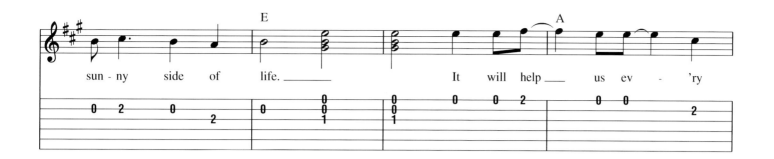

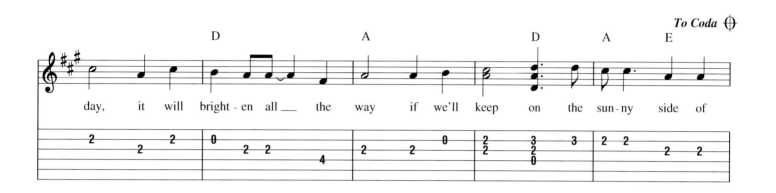

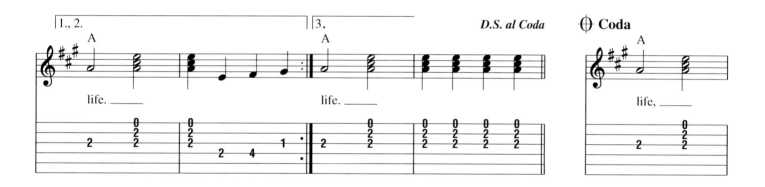

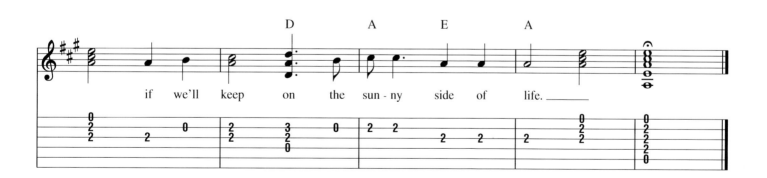

Additional Lyrics

2. Though the storm and its furies rage today,
Crushing hope that we cherish so dear,
The cloud and storm will in time pass away
And the sun again will shine bright and clear.

3. Let us greet with a song of hope each day,
Though the moment be cloudy or fair,
And let us trust in our Savior always,
He'll keep us ev'ryone in His care.

Down to the River to Pray

Traditional

Strum Pattern: 10
Pick Pattern: 10

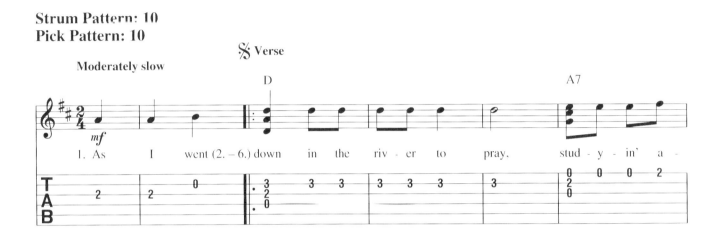

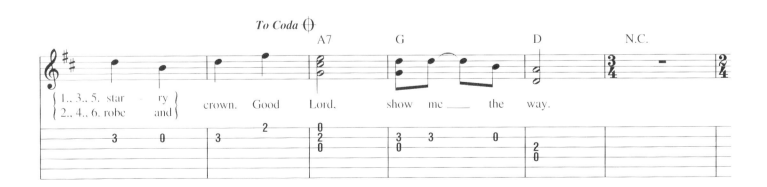

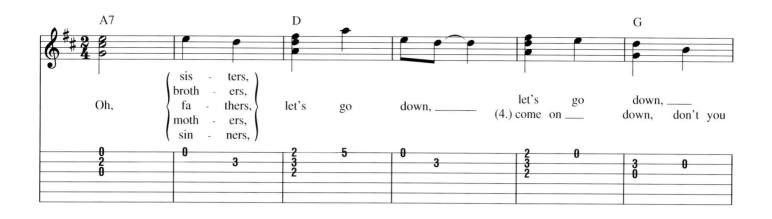

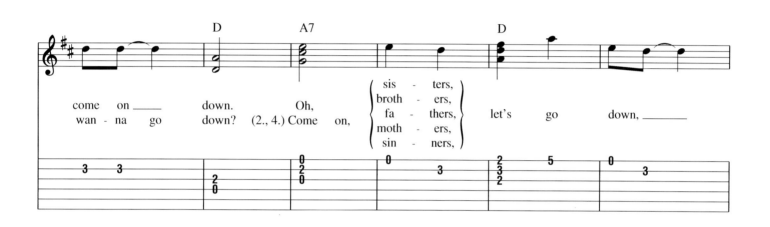

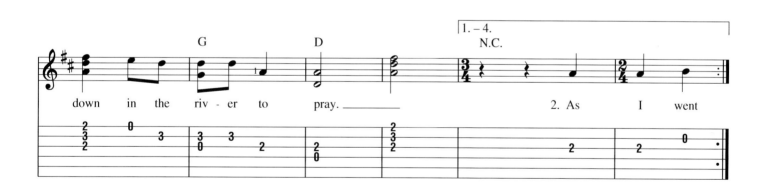

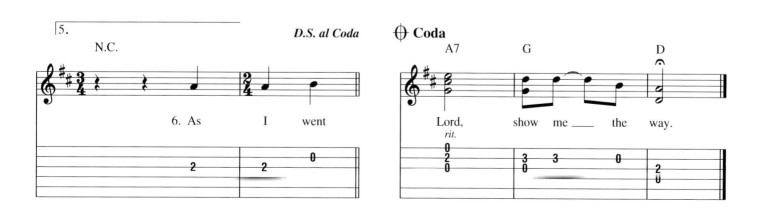

I Am a Man of Constant Sorrow

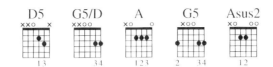

Words and Music by Carter Stanley

D5   G5/D   A   G5   Asus2

Strum Pattern: 3, 5
Pick Pattern: 1, 4

Intro
Moderately fast Country

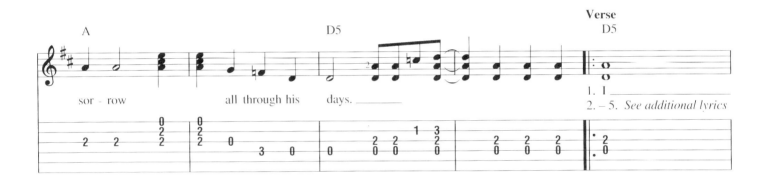

In con - stant

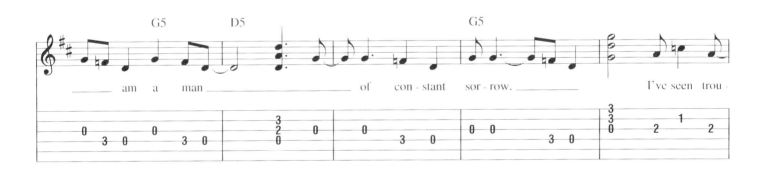

sor - row   all through his   days. _____

Verse

1. I _____
2. – 5. *See additional lyrics*

_____ am a   man _____   of   con - stant   sor - row.   I've seen trou-

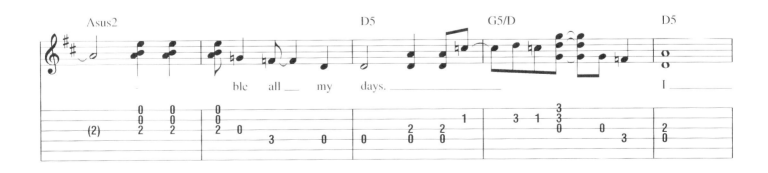

ble   all ___   my   days.   I

bid fare - well _____ to old ___ Ken - tuck - y, _____

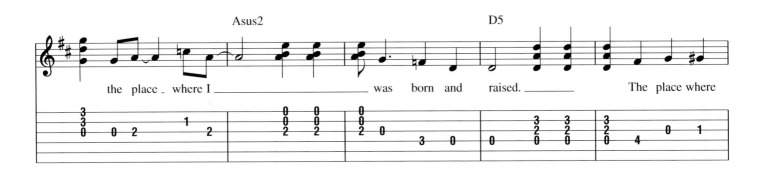

the place _ where I _____ was born and raised. _____ The place where

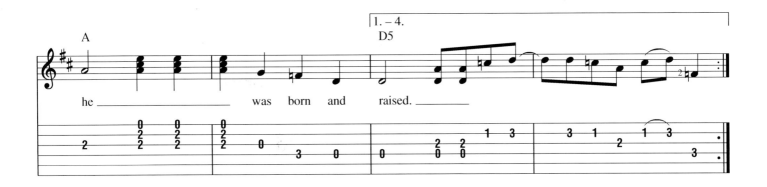

he _____ was born and raised. _____

shore. _____

Additional Lyrics

2. For six long years I've been in trouble,
No pleasure here on earth I've found.
For in this world I'm bound to ramble;
I have no friends to help me now.
He has no friends to help him now.

3. It's fare thee well, my own true lover,
I never expect to see you again,
For I'm bound to ride that Northern railroad;
Perhaps I'll die upon this train.
Perhaps he'll die upon this train.

4. You can bury me in some deep valley,
For many years where I may lay,
And you may learn to love another
While I am sleeping in my grave.
While he is sleeping in his grave.

5. Maybe your friends think I'm just a stranger;
My face, you never will see no more.
But there is one promise that is given:
I'll meet you on God's golden shore.
He'll meet you on God's golden shore.

I'll Fly Away

Words and Music by Albert E. Brumley

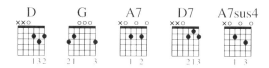

Strum Pattern: 3, 4
Pick Pattern: 1, 3

Intro-Mandolin Solo
Moderately

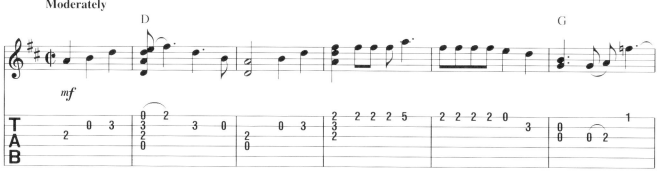

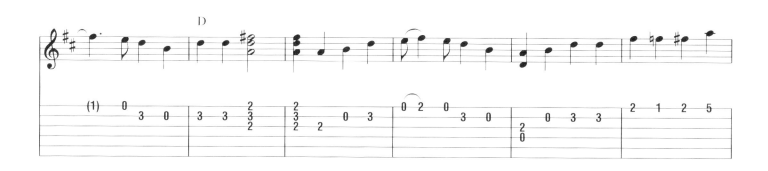

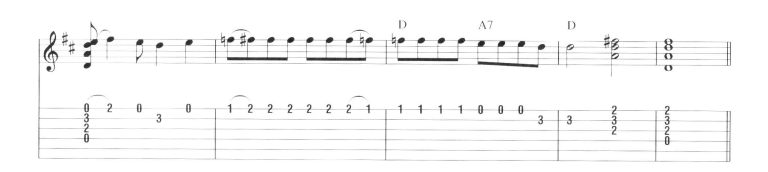

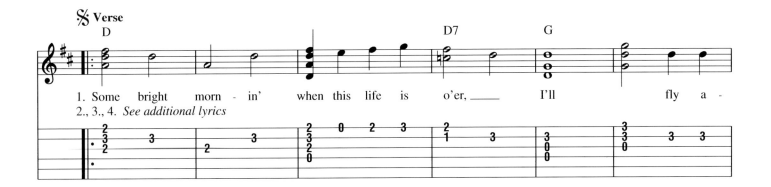

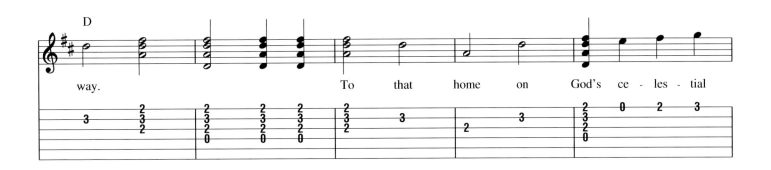

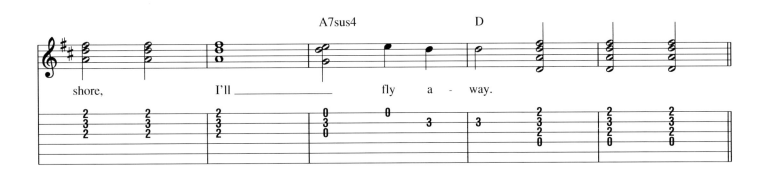

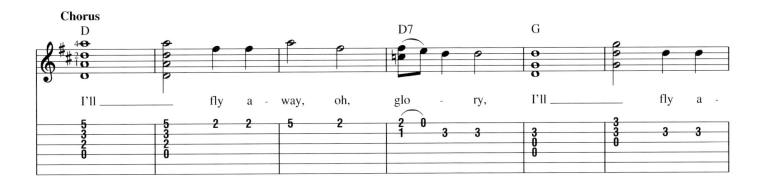

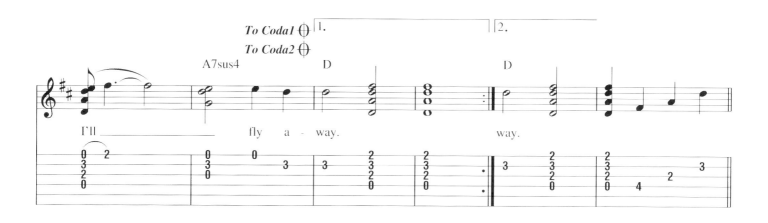

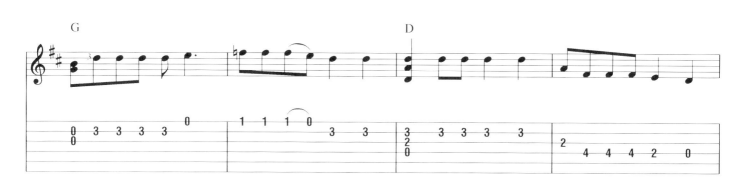

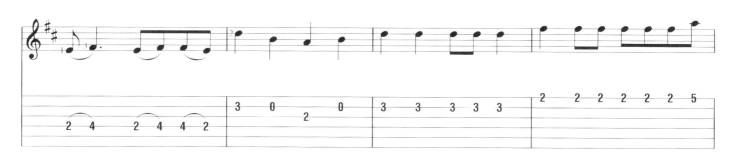

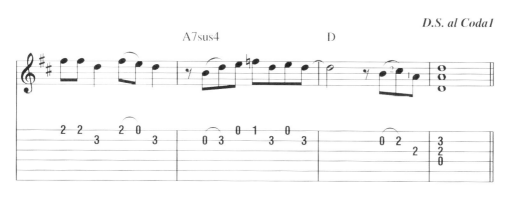

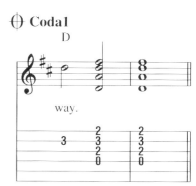

Chorus

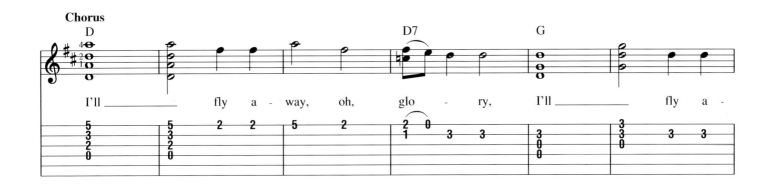

I'll _____ fly a - way, oh, glo - ry, I'll _____ fly a -

way in the morn - in'. When I die, hal - le - lu - jah by __ and by,

D.S. al Coda2 ⊕ **Coda2**

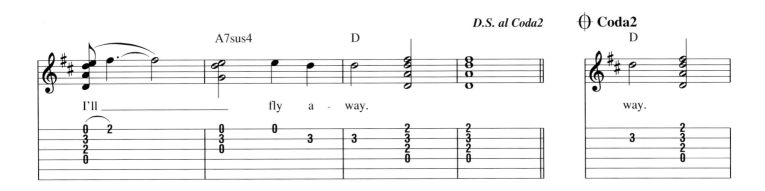

I'll _____ fly a - way.

way.

I'll _____ fly a - way.

Additional Lyrics

2. When the shadows of this life have gone,
I'll fly away.
Like a bird from these prison walls I'll fly.
I'll fly away.

3. Oh, how glad and happy when we meet.
I'll fly away.
No more cold iron shackles on my feet.
I'll fly away.

Didn't Leave Nobody But the Baby

Words and Music by Gillian Welch, T-Bone Burnett, Alan Lomax and Mrs. Sidney Carter

Strum Pattern: 4
Pick Pattern: 4

*Use Pattern 10

Additional Lyrics

2. Go to sleep, you little baby,
   Go to sleep, you little baby.
   Everybody's gone in the cotton and the corn,
   Didn't leave nobody but the baby.

3. You're sweet, little baby,
   You're sweet, little baby.
   Honey in the rock and the sugar don't stop,
   Gonna bring a bottle to the baby.

4. Don't you weep, pretty baby,
   Don't you weep, pretty baby.
   She's long gone with her red shoes on,
   Gonna need another lovin' baby.

5. Go to sleep, little baby,
   Go to sleep, little baby.
   You and me and the devil makes three,
   Don't need no other lovin' baby.

6. Go to sleep, you little baby,
   Go to sleep, you little baby.
   Come lay your bones on the alabaster stones
   And be my ever-lovin' baby.

In the Jailhouse Now

Words and Music by Jimmie Rodgers

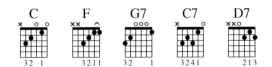

Strum Pattern: 2, 3
Pick Pattern: 3, 4

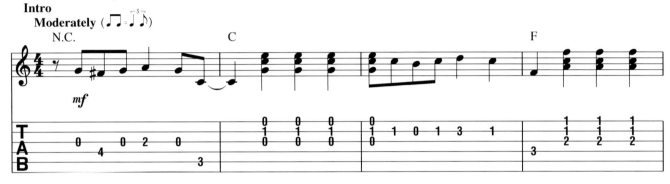

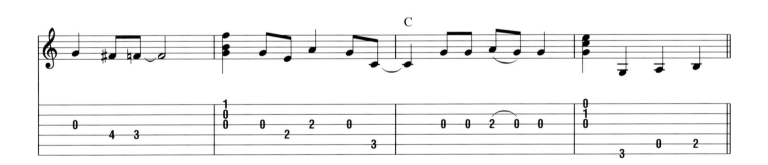

Verse

1. I had a friend _ named Ram - bl - in' Bob. _____ He used to steal, ____
2., 3. *See additional lyrics*

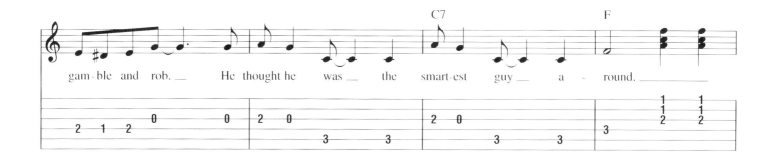

gam-ble and rob. ___ He thought he was ___ the smart-est guy ___ a - round. _____

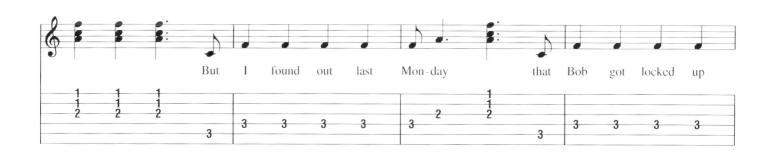

But I found out last Mon-day that Bob got locked up

Sun-day. They've got him in ___ the jail - house way down town. _____

Chorus

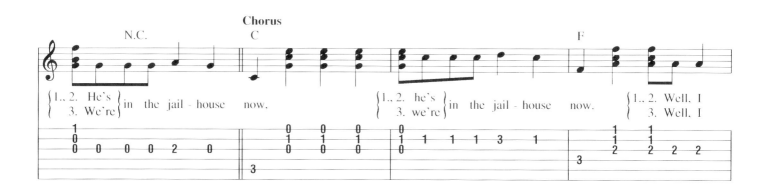

{1., 2. He's
3. We're} in the jail - house now.   {1., 2. he's
3. we're} in the jail - house now.   {1., 2. Well, I
3. Well, I

told him once or twice ___ to stop play-in' cards ___ and a - shoot-in' dice. ___
told that judge right to his face _____ I don't like to see this place. ___

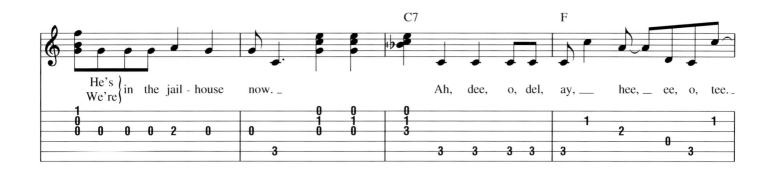

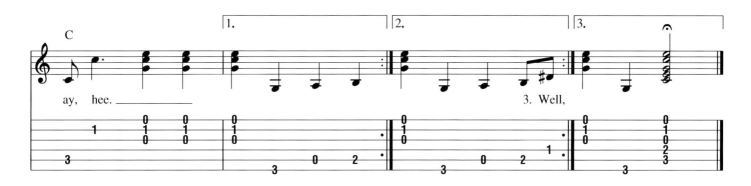

Additional Lyrics

2. Bob liked to play his poker,
   Pinochle, whist, and euchre,
   But shootin' dice was his fav'rite game.
   Well, he got throwed in jail
   With nobody to go his bail.
   The judge done said that he refused the fine.

3. Well, I went out last Tuesday.
   I met a girl name Susie.
   I said I was the swellest guy around.
   Well, we started to spendin' my money.
   And she started to callin' me honey.
   We took in ev'ry cabaret in town.

In the Highways
(I'll Be Somewhere Working for My Lord)

Words and Music by Maybelle Carter

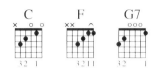

Strum Pattern: 3, 4
Pick Pattern: 3, 4

Intro
Moderately fast

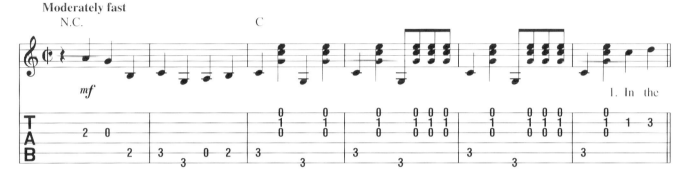

1. In the

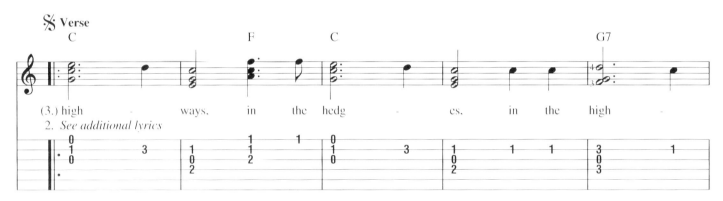

(3.) high - ways, in the hedg - es, in the high
2. *See additional lyrics*

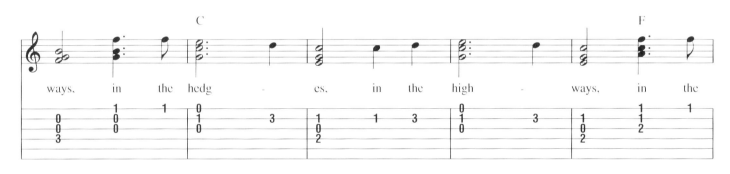

ways, in the hedg - es, in the high ways, in the

hedg - es, I'll be some-where a - work - ing for my Lord. _____ I'll be

Chorus

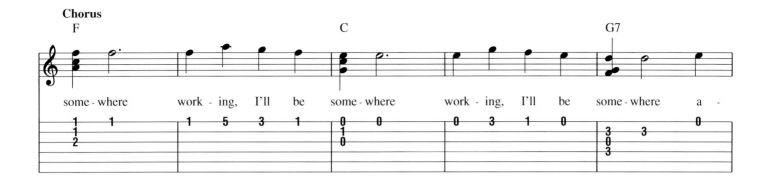

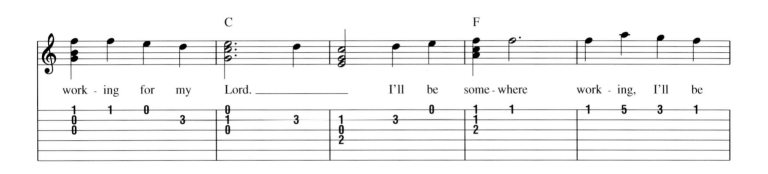

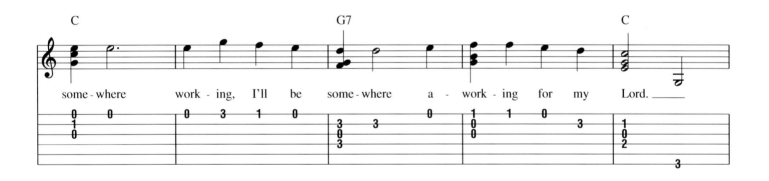

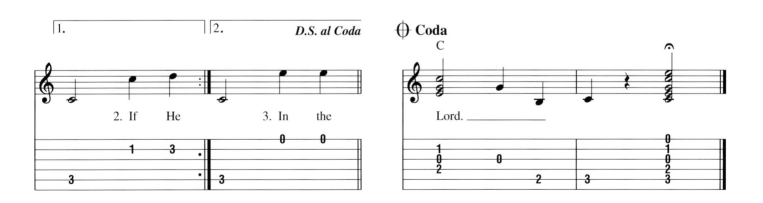

Additional Lyrics

2. If He calls me, I will answer,
   If He calls me, I will answer,
   If He calls me, I will answer.
   I'll be somewhere a-working for my Lord.

I Am Weary
(Let Me Rest)

Words and Music by Pete (Roberts) Kuykendall

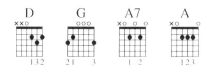

Strum Pattern: 2, 3
Pick Pattern: 3, 4

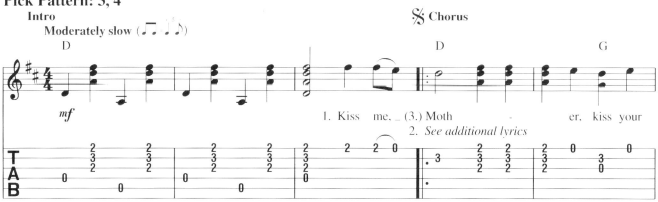

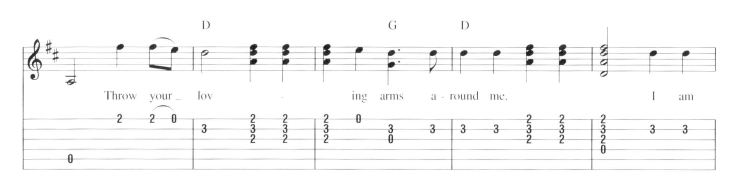

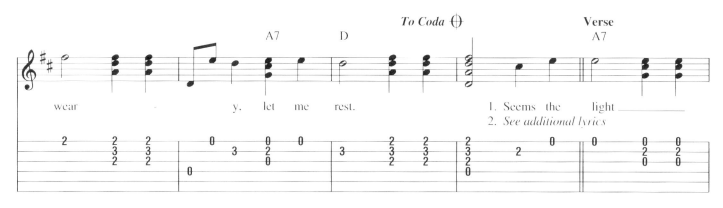

is — swift-ly fad - ing. _____ Bright - er scenes _____ they do — now

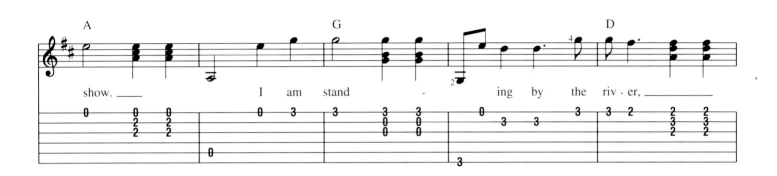

show. ____ I am stand - ing by the riv - er, _____

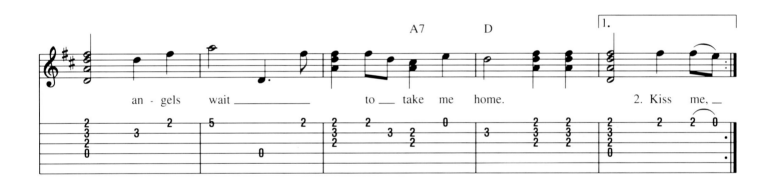

an - gels wait _____ to — take me home. 2. Kiss me, —

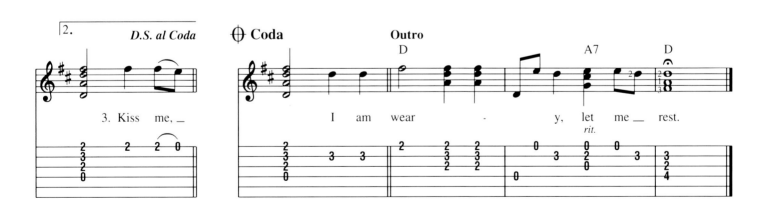

3. Kiss me, —   I am wear - y, let me — rest.

Additional Lyrics

Chorus 2. Kiss me, Mother, kiss your darlin'.
See the pain upon my brow.
While I'll soon be with the angels,
Fate has doomed my future now.

2. Through the years you've always loved me,
And my life you've tried to save.
But now I shall slumber sweetly
In a deep and lonely grave.

Angel Band

Words and Music by Ralph Stanley

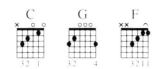

Strum Pattern: 7, 8

Pick Pattern: 7, 8

Intro

Moderate Country

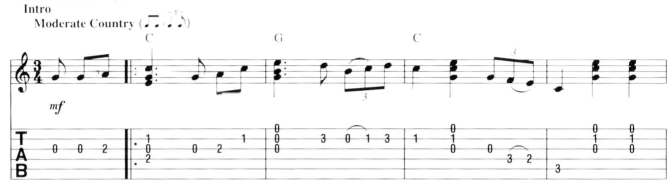

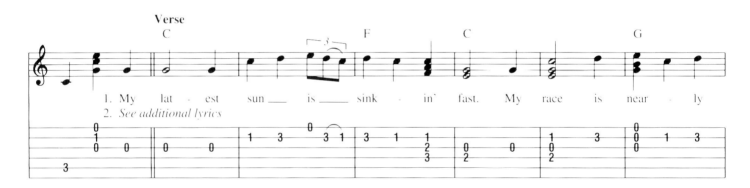

1. My lat-est sun is sink-in' fast. My race is near-ly run.
2. *See additional lyrics*

My strong-est tri-als now are past. My

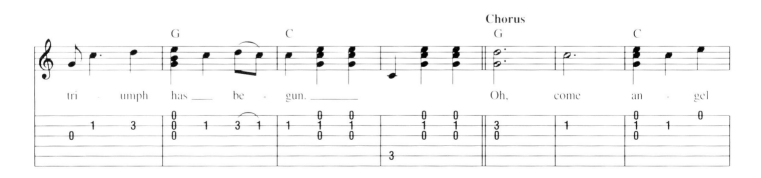

tri-umph has be-gun. Oh, come an-gel

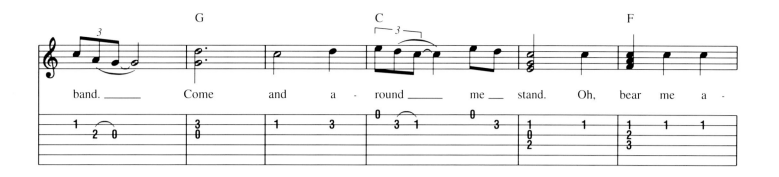

band. _____ Come and a - round _____ me _ stand. Oh, bear me a -

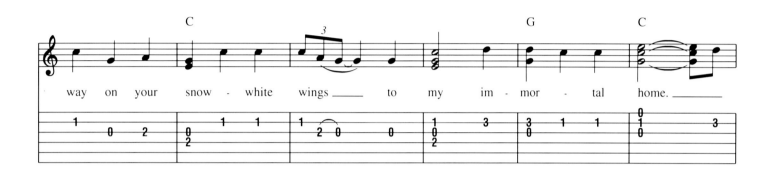

way on your snow - white wings _____ to my im - mor - tal home. _____

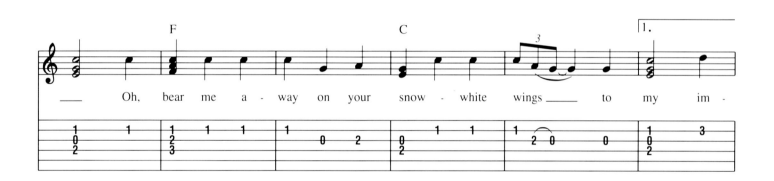

_____ Oh, bear me a - way on your snow - white wings _____ to my im -

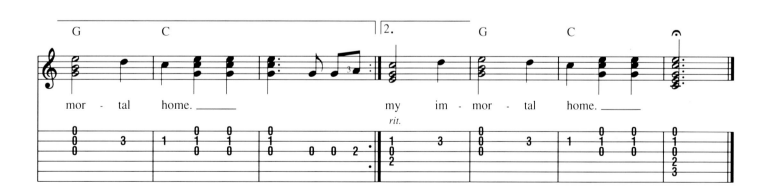

mor - tal home. _____ my im - mor - tal home. _____

rit.

Additional Lyrics

2. Oh, bear my longin' heart to Him
   Who bled and died for me,
   Whose blood now cleanses from all sin
   And gives me victory.

EASY GUITAR WITH NOTES & TAB

This series features simplified arrangements with notes, tab, chord charts, and strum and pick patterns.

MIXED FOLIOS

00702287	Acoustic	$16.99
00702002	Acoustic Rock Hits for Easy Guitar	$14.99
00702166	All-Time Best Guitar Collection	$19.99
00702232	Best Acoustic Songs for Easy Guitar	$14.99
00119835	Best Children's Songs	$16.99
00702233	Best Hard Rock Songs	$14.99
00703055	The Big Book of Nursery Rhymes & Children's Songs	$16.99
00322179	The Big Easy Book of Classic Rock Guitar	$24.95
00698978	Big Christmas Collection	$17.99
00702394	Bluegrass Songs for Easy Guitar	$12.99
00703387	Celtic Classics	$14.99
00224808	Chart Hits of 2016-2017	$14.99
00702149	Children's Christian Songbook	$9.99
00702237	Christian Acoustic Favorites	$12.95
00702028	Christmas Classics	$8.99
00101779	Christmas Guitar	$14.99
00702185	Christmas Hits	$10.99
00702141	Classic Rock	$8.95
00702203	CMT's 100 Greatest Country Songs	$27.95
00702283	The Contemporary Christian Collection	$16.99

00702239	Country Classics for Easy Guitar	$19.99
00702282	Country Hits of 2009–2010	$14.99
00702257	Easy Acoustic Guitar Songs	$14.99
00702280	Easy Guitar Tab White Pages	$29.99
00702041	Favorite Hymns for Easy Guitar	$10.99
00140841	4-Chord Hymns for Guitar	$9.99
00702281	4 Chord Rock	$10.99
00126894	Frozen	$14.99
00702286	Glee	$16.99
00699374	Gospel Favorites	$16.99
00122138	The Grammy Awards® Record of the Year 1958-2011	$19.99
00702160	The Great American Country Songbook	$16.99
00702050	Great Classical Themes for Easy Guitar	$8.99
00702116	Greatest Hymns for Guitar	$10.99
00702184	Guitar Instrumentals	$9.95
00148030	Halloween Guitar Songs	$14.99
00702273	Irish Songs	$12.99
00702275	Jazz Favorites for Easy Guitar	$15.99
00702274	Jazz Standards for Easy Guitar	$15.99
00702162	Jumbo Easy Guitar Songbook	$19.99
00702258	Legends of Rock	$14.99

00702189	MTV's 100 Greatest Pop Songs	$24.95
00702272	1950s Rock	$15.99
00702271	1960s Rock	$15.99
00702270	1970s Rock	$15.99
00702269	1980s Rock	$15.99
00702268	1990s Rock	$15.99
00109725	Once	$14.99
00702187	Selections from O Brother Where Art Thou?	$17.99
00702178	100 Songs for Kids	$14.99
00702515	Pirates of the Caribbean	$14.99
00702125	Praise and Worship for Guitar	$10.99
00702285	Southern Rock Hits	$12.99
00121535	30 Easy Celtic Guitar Solos	$14.99
00702220	Today's Country Hits	$9.95
00121900	Today's Women of Pop & Rock	$14.99
00283786	Top Hits of 2018	$14.99
00702294	Top Worship Hits	$15.99
00702255	VH1's 100 Greatest Hard Rock Songs	$27.99
00702175	VH1's 100 Greatest Songs of Rock and Roll	$24.99
00702253	Wicked	$12.99

ARTIST COLLECTIONS

00702267	AC/DC for Easy Guitar	$15.99
00702598	Adele for Easy Guitar	$15.99
00702040	Best of the Allman Brothers	$15.99
00702865	J.S. Bach for Easy Guitar	$14.99
00702169	Best of The Beach Boys	$12.99
00702292	The Beatles — 1	$19.99
00125796	Best of Chuck Berry	$14.99
00702201	The Essential Black Sabbath	$12.95
02501615	Zac Brown Band — The Foundation	$16.99
02501621	Zac Brown Band — You Get What You Give	$16.99
00702043	Best of Johnny Cash	$16.99
00702090	Eric Clapton's Best	$12.99
00702086	Eric Clapton — from the Album Unplugged	$10.95
00702202	The Essential Eric Clapton	$14.99
00702250	blink-182 — Greatest Hits	$15.99
00702053	Best of Patsy Cline	$14.99
00702229	The Very Best of Creedence Clearwater Revival	$15.99
00702145	Best of Jim Croce	$15.99
00702278	Crosby, Stills & Nash	$12.99
00702219	David Crowder*Band Collection	$12.95
14042809	Bob Dylan	$14.99
00702276	Fleetwood Mac — Easy Guitar Collection	$14.99
00139462	The Very Best of Grateful Dead	$15.99
00702136	Best of Merle Haggard	$12.99
00702227	Jimi Hendrix — Smash Hits	$14.99
00702288	Best of Hillsong United	$12.99
00702236	Best of Antonio Carlos Jobim	$14.99
00702245	Elton John — Greatest Hits 1970–2002	$14.99

00129855	Jack Johnson	$15.99
00702204	Robert Johnson	$10.99
00702234	Selections from Toby Keith — 35 Biggest Hits	$12.95
00702003	Kiss	$10.99
00110578	Best of Kutless	$12.99
00702216	Lynyrd Skynyrd	$15.99
00702182	The Essential Bob Marley	$14.94
00146081	Maroon 5	$14.99
00121925	Bruno Mars – Unorthodox Jukebox	$12.99
00702248	Paul McCartney — All the Best	$14.99
00702129	Songs of Sarah McLachlan	$12.95
00125484	The Best of MercyMe	$12.99
02501316	Metallica — Death Magnetic	$19.99
00702209	Steve Miller Band — Young Hearts (Greatest Hits)	$12.95
00124167	Jason Mraz	$15.99
00702096	Best of Nirvana	$15.99
00702211	The Offspring — Greatest Hits	$12.95
00138026	One Direction	$14.99
00702030	Best of Roy Orbison	$14.99
00702144	Best of Ozzy Osbourne	$14.99
00702279	Tom Petty	$12.99
00102911	Pink Floyd	$16.99
00702139	Elvis Country Favorites	$14.99
00702293	The Very Best of Prince	$15.99
00699415	Best of Queen for Guitar	$14.99
00109279	Best of R.E.M.	$14.99
00702208	Red Hot Chili Peppers — Greatest Hits	$14.99

00198960	The Rolling Stones	$16.99
00174793	The Very Best of Santana	$14.99
00702196	Best of Bob Seger	$12.95
00146046	Ed Sheeran	$14.99
00702252	Frank Sinatra — Nothing But the Best	$12.99
00702010	Best of Rod Stewart	$16.99
00702049	Best of George Strait	$14.99
00702259	Taylor Swift for Easy Guitar	$15.99
00702260	Taylor Swift — Fearless	$14.99
00139727	Taylor Swift — 1989	$17.99
00115960	Taylor Swift — Red	$16.99
00253667	Taylor Swift — Reputation	$17.99
00702290	Taylor Swift — Speak Now	$15.99
00702226	Chris Tomlin — See the Morning	$12.95
00148643	Train	$14.99
00702427	U2 — 18 Singles	$16.99
00702108	Best of Stevie Ray Vaughan	$16.99
00702123	Best of Hank Williams	$14.99
00702111	Stevie Wonder — Guitar Collection	$9.95
00702228	Neil Young — Greatest Hits	$15.99
00119133	Neil Young — Harvest	$14.99
00702188	Essential ZZ Top	$14.99

Prices, contents and availability subject to change without notice